T0103117

Exploring Coral Reefs

Anita Ganeri

Heinemann
LIBRARY
Chicago, Illinois

© 2014 Heinemann Library
an imprint of Capstone Global Library, LLC
Chicago, Illinois

To contact Capstone Global Library please phone 800-747-4992, or visit our web site, www.capstonepub.com

All rights reserved. No part of this publication may be reproduced or transmitted in any form or by any means, electronic or mechanical, including photocopying, recording, taping, or any information storage and retrieval system, without permission in writing from the publisher.

Edited by Dan Nunn, Rebecca Rissman, and Helen Cox Cannons
Designed by Joanna Hinton-Malivoire
Original illustrations © Capstone Global Library Ltd
Illustrated by Sernur ISIK
Picture research by Mica Brancic
Production by Helen McCreath
Originated by Capstone Global Library Ltd

17 16 15 14 13
10 9 8 7 6 5 4 3 2 1

Library of Congress Cataloging-in-Publication Data
Ganeri, Anita, 1961- author.
Exploring coral reefs : a Benjamin Blog and his inquisitive dog investigation / Anita Ganeri.
pages cm.—(Exploring habitats, with Benjamin Blog and his inquisitive dog)
Includes bibliographical references and index.
ISBN 978-1-4329-8780-0 (hb)—ISBN 978-1-4329-8787-9 (pb) 1. Coral reef ecology—Juvenile literature. 2. Coral reefs and islands—Juvenile literature. 3. Coral reef animals—Juvenile literature. I. Title.

QH541.5.C7G36 2014
551.42'4—dc23 2013017421

Image Credits
Alamy: imageBROKER.com/GmbH & Co. KG, 16, Reinhard Dirscherl, 18; Getty Images: Brett Monroe Garner, 26, johnandersonphoto, cover, Sean Scott, 24; Shutterstock: Dudarev Mikhail, 4, icemanphotos, 9, Ingvars Birznieks, 22, James A Dawson, 20, Kristina Vackova, 23, Krzysztof Odziomek, 13, Olga Khoroshunova, 21, Pinosub, 7, R Gombarik, 11, Rich Carey, 10, 17, 29 (top), Richard Whitcombe, 5, Sergey Skleznev, 15, stephan kerkhofs, 14, tae208, 27, 29 (bottom), tororo reaction, 8, 25, Tyler Fox, 6, V_E, 12, 19

We would like to thank Michael Bright for his invaluable help in the preparation of this book.

Every effort has been made to contact copyright holders of any material reproduced in this book. Any omissions will be rectified in subsequent printings if notice is given to the publisher.

All the Internet addresses (URLs) given in this book were valid at the time of going to press. However, due to the dynamic nature of the Internet, some addresses may have changed, or sites may have changed or ceased to exist since publication. While the author and publisher regret any inconvenience this may cause readers, no responsibility for any such changes can be accepted by either the author or the publisher.

Some words are shown in bold, **like this**. You can find out what they mean by looking in the glossary.

Printed in the United States 6100

Contents

Welcome to Coral Reefs! 4

Coral Builders 6

Ready, Steady, Grow 8

Daisies, Mushrooms, and Brains 10

Fabulous Fish 12

Night Hunters 16

Living Together 20

Slugs and Shells 22

Remarkable Reef 24

Coral Catastrophe 26

Remarkable Coral Reefs Quiz 28

Glossary *30*

Find Out More *31*

Index *32*

Welcome to Coral Reefs!

Hello! My name's Benjamin Blog and this is Barko Polo, my **inquisitive** dog. (He's named after the ancient ace explorer **Marco Polo**.) We have just returned from our latest adventure—exploring **coral reefs** around the world. We put this book together from some of the blog posts we wrote on the way.

BARKO'S BLOG-TASTIC CORAL REEF FACTS

Coral reefs are the richest **habitats** in the ocean. They are home to thousands of creatures, from clown fish and porcupine fish, to giant clams, sea cucumbers, and sharks.

Coral Builders

Posted by: Ben Blog | June 3 at 9:13 a.m.

Coral reefs are amazing places, and I couldn't wait to dive in. First, I wanted to find out how reefs are made. They are built by millions of tiny sea creatures, called coral **polyps**. The polyps grow hard cases around their bodies. When they die, the cases are left behind.

BARKO'S BLOG-TASTIC CORAL REEF FACTS

Coral polyps belong to the same family as sea anemones. Like sea anemones, polyps have stinging **tentacles**. They wave their tentacles in the water to catch tiny creatures to eat.

Ready, Steady, Grow

Posted by: Ben Blog | July 11 at 2:45 p.m.

Tropical coral reefs grow along the coast in tropical oceans. They like warm, clean, shallow water—that's fine for me, too! Tiny plants, called **algae**, live inside some polyps' bodies and help the **polyps** make their hard cases. The algae need plenty of sunlight to make their own food.

BARKO'S BLOG-TASTIC CORAL REEF FACTS

Atolls, like this one, are tiny **coral** islands. They start as reefs growing around volcanoes that poked up from the ocean floor. Slowly, the volcanoes sink, leaving the atolls behind.

Daisies, Mushrooms, and Brains

Posted by: Ben Blog | August 18 at 7:52 p.m.

I've reached the main part of the reef and counted 10 types of **coral** already. There are many different sizes and shapes. There are corals that look like daisies, mushrooms, and deer antlers. This is brain coral. It can grow to 6½ feet (2 meters) across. Can you guess how it got its name?

BARKO'S BLOG-TASTIC CORAL REEF FACTS

When coral is alive, it's brightly colored—pink, blue, purple, yellow, and green. Dead coral is chalky white.

Fabulous Fish

Posted by: Ben Blog | September 3 at 11:25 a.m.

It's daytime on the reef, and there are fabulous fish everywhere. In fact, more types of fish make their home on **coral reefs** than anywhere else in the ocean. I took this photo of a **school** of butterfly fish. Their bright colors help them spot each other in the crowd.

BARKO'S BLOG-TASTIC CORAL REEF FACTS

The parrot fish gets its name from its sharp, beak-like teeth. Its beak is perfect for crunching on coral and scraping **algae** from the rocks to eat.

Coral reefs are crowded places, so fish and other creatures take turns to feed. Some fish come out in the daytime. Other fish come out at night. In the day, these soldierfish hide in holes in the **coral**. At night, they use their large eyes to find food in the dark.

BARKO'S BLOG-TASTIC CORAL REEF FACTS

If a **predator** tries to attack a lionfish, it's in for a painful surprise. The lionfish's feathery fins are covered in poisonous spines that it jabs into its enemy. Ouch!

Night Hunters

Posted by: Ben Blog | October 16 at 10:59 p.m.

Tonight we went on another night dive. This time, I was searching for sharks. Whitetip reef sharks are expert hunters. They can sniff out fish hiding in cracks in the **coral** and wriggle inside to get them out. They can also pick up tiny bleeps of electricity that fish give out when they swim.

BARKO'S BLOG-TASTIC CORAL REEF FACTS

A moray eel hides in its hole, with just its head poking out. Its mouth is lined with large, razor-sharp teeth for catching any passing fish, squid, and crabs.

Danger lurks around every corner on a **coral reef**. Some reef creatures have special ways of staying alive. Stonefish sit on the ocean floor. They look like weed-covered rocks. But they also have sharp spines on their back for shooting deadly venom, or liquid poison, into their enemies.

BARKO'S BLOG-TASTIC CORAL REEF FACTS

Surgeonfish have two sharp, spike-like spines on either side of their tail. If a fish is attacked, its spines stick out and it swipes its tail from side to side.

Living Together

Posted by: Ben Blog | December 5 at 12:36 p.m.

Back in the water, I'm watching a moray eel getting its teeth cleaned by tiny shrimps, called cleaner shrimps. The huge eel could easily eat the shrimps, but it stays quite still while they pick dead **scales**, fungus, and bits of leftover food from its skin and sharp teeth.

BARKO'S BLOG-TASTIC CORAL REEF FACTS

A clown fish lives among the stinging **tentacles** of a sea anemone. This keeps it safe from enemies. The fish does not get stung because its body is covered in special slime.

Slugs and Shells

Posted by: Ben Blog | January 14 at 1:24 p.m.

As I was heading back up to the boat, I spotted this super-sized shell. It's a giant clam, the biggest seashell in the world! It can measure more than 3 feet (1 meter) across and weigh more than 500 pounds (227 kilograms). The blue color on its lips is caused by tiny **algae**.

BARKO'S BLOG-TASTIC CORAL REEF FACTS

On land, slugs are plain brown or black, but sea slugs, like this Spanish dancer, have amazing colors, frills, and pointed **tentacles**. Their colors are a warning that they are poisonous!

Remarkable Reef

Posted by: Ben Blog | February 12 at 4:01 p.m.

The last stop on our trip was the Great Barrier Reef in Australia—the world's largest **coral reef**. It's home to thousands of astonishing animals, including 1,500 types of fish, 400 types of **coral**, 4,000 types of **mollusks**, and some rare **reptiles**, like this loggerhead turtle.

BARKO'S BLOG-TASTIC CORAL REEF FACTS

The Great Barrier Reef is more than 1,250 miles (2,000 kilometers) long. It's made up of thousands of smaller reefs and hundreds of tiny islands. It's so huge that it can be seen from outer space.

Coral Catastrophe

Posted by: Ben Blog | February 13 at 8:15 a.m.

All over the world, **coral reefs** are in danger. They are being damaged by **pollution**, shell and coral collectors, and companies drilling for oil. Huge patches of coral are turning white and dying. This is called coral **bleaching**. It happens when the ocean gets too salty or warm.

BARKO'S BLOG-TASTIC CORAL REEF FACTS

This odd-looking creature is a crown-of-thorns starfish. They have up to 20 arms and are covered in thick spines. They have eaten and killed enormous chunks of the Great Barrier Reef.

Remarkable Coral Reefs Quiz

If you are planning your own **coral reef** expedition, you need to be prepared. Find out how much you know about remarkable reefs with our quick quiz.

1. Which creatures build coral reefs?
a) reef sharks
b) coral **polyps**
c) sea anemones

2. What color is dead **coral**?
a) white
b) black
c) purple

3. Which fish have two spines on their tail?
a) lionfish
b) butterfly fish
c) surgeonfish

4. Where does a clown fish live?
a) in a hole in the coral
b) in a sea anemone
c) in a giant clam

5. How big is a giant clam?
a) 3 feet across
b) 30 feet across
c) 300 feet across

6. Where is the world's biggest reef?
a) India
b) Australia
c) Egypt

7. What is this?

8. What is this?

Answers
1. b
2. a
3. c
4. b
5. a
6. b
7. brain coral
8. crown-of-thorns starfish

Glossary

algae tiny plant-like living thing

bleaching turning white

coral rock-like material made by tiny sea creatures

coral reef long structure made from coral that grows along the coast

habitat place where animals and plants live

inquisitive interested in learning about the world

Marco Polo explorer who lived from about 1254 to 1324. He traveled from Italy to China.

mollusk animal, such as a slug, snail, clam, or mussel

pollution things that make a place dirty or damage it, such as litter, oil, and chemicals

polyp tiny sea creature that makes coral reefs

predator animal that hunts and kills other animals for food

reptile cold-blooded animal that has scaly skin and lays eggs on land. Reptiles include snakes and lizards.

scale tiny flap covering a fish's body

school large group of fish, swimming together

tentacle long, waving body part that some sea creatures use to catch food

tropical found in warm parts of the world

Find Out More

Books

Ganeri, Anita. *Ocean Divers.* Chicago: Raintree, 2012.

Llewellyn, Claire. *Oceans (Habitat Survival).* Chicago: Raintree, 2013.

Murphy, Julie. *Ocean Animal Adaptations.* Mankato, Minn.: Capstone, 2012.

Salas, Laura Purdie. *Coral Reefs: Colorful Underwater Habitats.* Mankato, Minn.: Picture Window, 2009.

Web Sites

FactHound offers a safe, fun way to find Internet sites related to this book. All of the sites on FactHound have been researched by our staff.

Here's all you do:
Visit www.facthound.com
Type in this code: 9781432987800

Index

algae 8, 13, 22, 30
atolls 9
Australia 24

bleaching 26, 30
brain coral 10
butterfly fish 12

clams, giant 5, 22
cleaner shrimps 20
clown fish 5, 21
colors 11, 12, 23
coral islands 9, 25
crabs 17
crown-of-thorns starfish 27

dead coral 11, 26

electricity 16

fungus 20

Great Barrier Reef 24–25

habitats 5, 30

largest coral reef 24
lionfish 15

Marco Polo 4, 30
mollusks 24, 30
moray eels 17, 20

parrot fish 13
poison 15, 18, 23
pollution 26, 30
polyps 6–7, 8, 30
porcupine fish 5
predators 15, 30

scales 20
school 12, 30
sea anemones 7, 21
sea cucumbers 5
sea slugs 23
sharks 5, 16
shells 22, 26
soldierfish 14
spines 15, 18, 19
squid 17
starfish 27
stonefish 18
surgeonfish 19

tentacles 7, 21, 23, 30
tropical oceans 8
turtles 24

volcanoes 9

whitetip reef sharks 16